Move him into the sun

Bob Chilcott

for upper voices, SATB, and piano (with snare drum,
tenor drum, and solo cello) or chamber orchestra

Vocal score

MUSIC DEPARTMENT

OXFORD
UNIVERSITY PRESS

OXFORD

UNIVERSITY PRESS

Great Clarendon Street, Oxford OX2 6DP,
United Kingdom

Oxford University Press is a department of the University of Oxford.
It furthers the University's objective of excellence in research, scholarship,
and education by publishing worldwide. Oxford is a registered trade mark of
Oxford University Press in the UK and in certain other countries

First published 2018

Impression: 1

ISBN 978-0-19-341082-4

Music origination by Katie Johnston
Printed in Great Britain on acid-free paper by
Halstan & Co. Ltd, Amersham, Bucks.

Contents

Composer's note

Wilfred Owen is known to many as the poet who died a young man, and who wrote so vividly and emotionally about the horror and futility of war. However, other passionate themes are ever-present in his poetry, the two principal ones perhaps being those of beauty and love, the latter not only for the natural world around him but also for his fellow human beings, comrades, and friends. In this piece the image of the sun, as a source of light, life, and energy, is the one that I have focused on. Portrayed here largely by the upper-voice choir, it ultimately becomes a source of redemption and an expression of feeling at one with life, articulated so beautifully in Owen's poetry.

Commissioned by the Trustees of the St Chad's Music Festival and Shrewsbury Bookfest in memory of Wilfred Owen, the Shropshire soldier-poet who was born in Oswestry on 18 March 1893, lived in Shrewsbury from 1907, and was killed in action near Ors in Northern France on 4 November 1918.

Duration: *c*.25 minutes

An accompaniment for small orchestra (2fl, ob, cl, bsn, hn in F, timp, perc (2 players), pno, str) is available on hire/rental from the publisher or appropriate agent. For orchestral performances, the piano part available on hire/rental should be used, rather than the part in the vocal score. The parts for percussion in movement two and solo cello in movement three are identical in the vocal score and orchestral set.

Texts

1. Song of Songs

Extract from 'The Promisers' (Upper voices)

When I awoke, the glancing day looked gay;
The air said: Fare you fleetly; you will meet him!
And when the prosp'rous sun was well begun
I heard a bird say: Sweetly you shall greet him!

'Song of Songs' (SATB)

Sing me at morn but only with your laugh;
Even as Spring that laugheth into leaf;
Even as Love that laugheth after Life.

Sing me but only with your speech all day,
As voluble leaflets do; let viols die;
The least word of your lips is melody!

Sing me at eve but only with your sigh!
Like lifting seas it solaceth; breathe so,
Slowly and low, the sense that no songs say.

Sing me at midnight with your murmurous heart!
Let youth's immortal-moaning chords be heard
Throbbing through you, and sobbing, unsubdued.

2. Spring Offensive

Extract from 'The Promisers' (Upper voices)

The sun felt strong and bold upon my shoulder;
It hung, it clung as it were my friend's arm.
The birds fifed on before, shrill-piping pipers,
Right down to town; and there they ceased to charm.

Extract from 'Spring Offensive' (SATB)

Hour after hour they ponder the warm field
And the far valley behind, where the buttercups
Had blessed with gold their slow boots coming up;
When even the little brambles would not yield,
But clutched and clung to them like sorrowing arms;
They breathe like trees unstirred.

Till like a cold gust thrills the little word
At which each body and its soul begird†
And tighten them for battle. No alarms
Of bugles, no high flags, no clamorous haste—
Only a lift and flare of eyes that faced
The sun, like a friend with whom their love is done.
O larger shone that smile against the sun—
Mightier than his whose bounty these have spurned.

† embrace; encompass

3. Apologia pro Poemate Meo

Extract from 'Apologia pro Poemate Meo'

I, too, saw God through mud—
The mud that cracked on cheeks when wretches smiled.
War brought more glory to their eyes than blood,
And gave their laughs more glee than shakes a child.

I, too, have dropped off Fear—
Behind the barrage, dead as my platoon,
And sailed my spirit surging light and clear
Past the entanglement where hopes lay strewn.

I have made fellowships—
Untold of happy lovers in old song.
For love is not the binding of fair lips
With the soft silk of eyes that look and long.

I have perceived much beauty
In the hoarse oaths that kept our courage straight;
Heard music in the silentness of duty;
Found peace where shell-storms spouted reddest spate.

4. Futility

Extract from 'Sonnet, To a child' (Upper voices)

To all men else uncouth;
Save me, who know your smile comes very old,
Learnt of the happy dead that laughed with gods;
For earlier suns than ours have lent you gold;
Sly fauns and trees have given you jigs and nods.

'Futility' (SATB)

Move him into the sun—
Gently its touch awoke him once,
At home, whispering of fields half-sown.
Always it woke him, even in France,
Until this morning and this snow.
If anything might rouse him now
The kind old sun will know.

Think how it wakes the seeds—
Woke, once, the clays of a cold star.
Are limbs, so dear achieved, are sides
Full-nerved—still warm—too hard to stir?
Was it for this the clay grew tall?
—O what made fatuous sunbeams toil
To break earth's sleep at all?

5. Winter Song

Extract from 'Winter Song'

From off your face, into the winds of winter,
The sun-brown and the summer-gold are blowing;
But they shall gleam again with spiritual glinter,
When paler beauty on your brows falls snowing,
And through those snows my looks shall be soft-going.

Extract from 'Happiness'

The sun may cleanse,
And time, and starlight. Life will sing sweet songs,
And gods will show us pleasure more than men's.

Texts from *Wilfred Owen: The War Poems*, ed. Jon Stallworthy (1935–2014) (Chatto & Windus, 1994).

Move him into the sun

Commissioned by the Trustees of the St Chad's Music Festival and Shrewsbury Bookfest in memory of Wilfred Owen

Move him into the sun

1. Song of Songs

Wilfred Owen (1893–1918)

BOB CHILCOTT

Printed in Great Britain

OXFORD UNIVESITY PRESS, MUSIC DEPARTMENT, GREAT CLARENDON STREET, OXFORD OX2 6DP

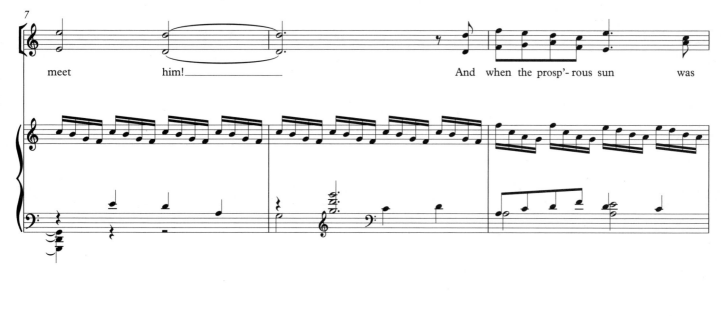

meet him!_____ And when the prosp'-rous sun was

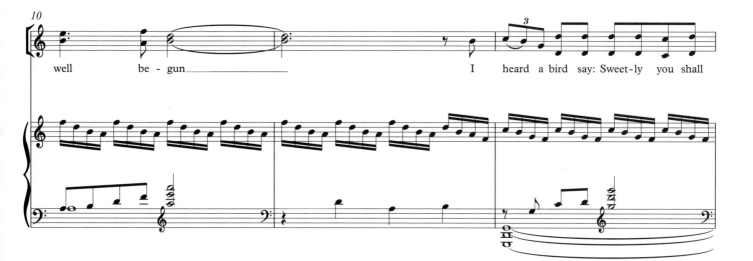

well be - gun_____ I heard a bird say: Sweet-ly you shall

greet him!_____

Sing me at morn but on-ly with your laugh;

E - ven as Spring that laugh-eth in - to leaf;

E - ven as Love that laugh-eth af - ter Life.

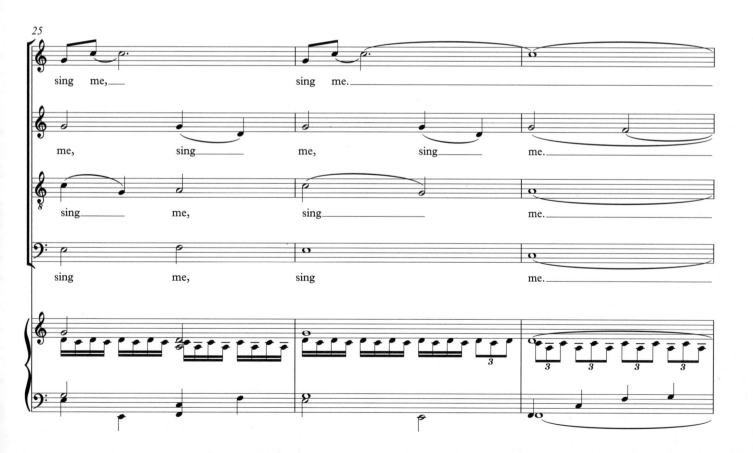

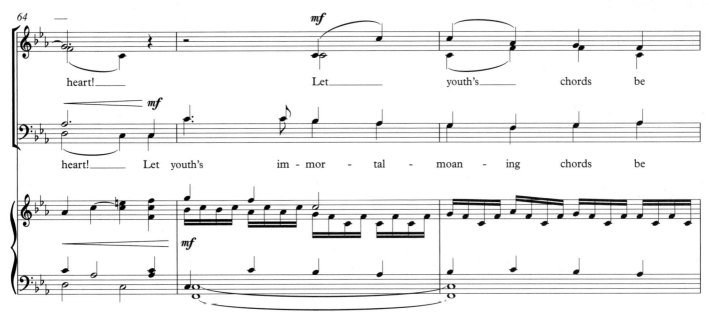

heart!_____ Let_____ youth's_____ chords be

heart!_____ Let youth's im - mor - tal - moan - ing chords be

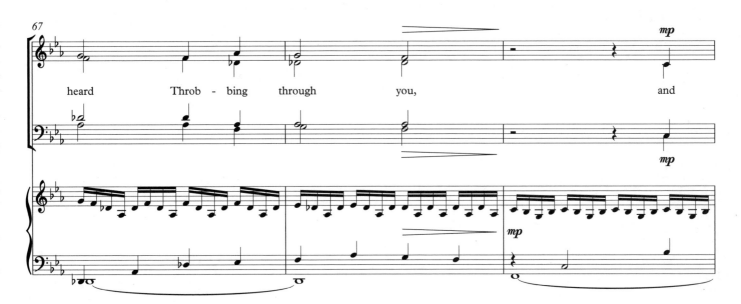

heard Throb - bing through you, and

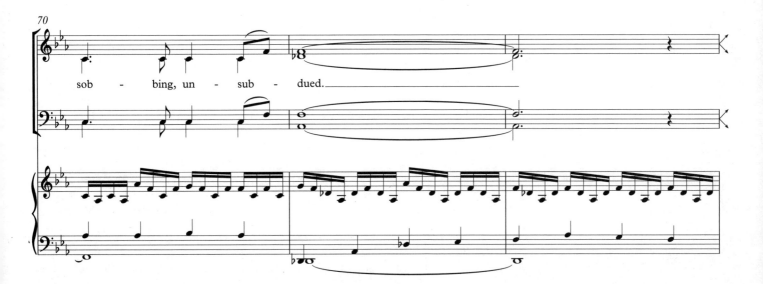

sob - bing, un - sub - dued._____

2. Spring Offensive

The sun felt strong and bold u-pon_ my shoul - der;_____ It hung, it clung as it were my_ friend's_ arm._____ The

birds fifed on be - fore,__ shrill - pi - ping pi - pers,_____ Right down to town; and there they ceased to

charm._____ Right down to town; and there they ceased to charm. The sun felt__

strong,_____ the sun felt__ strong,_____ the sun felt__

up.

yield, not yield.

yield, not yield.

yield, not yield. But clutched and clung to them like

sor - row - ing arms; They breathe like trees un - stirred.

SOPRANOS & ALTOS *unis.*

Till like a cold gust thrills the lit - tle word At which each bo - dy and its soul be - gird† And tight - en them for bat - tle.

No al - arms Of bu - gles,

No al - arms Of bu - gles,

No al - arms Of bu - gles,

† embrace; encompass

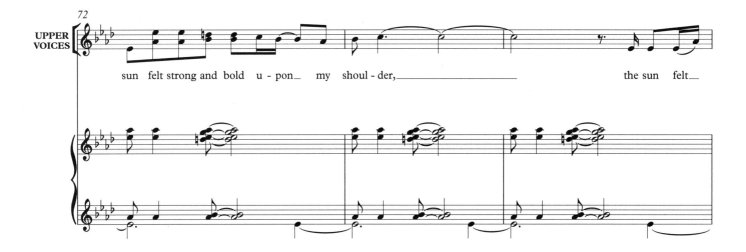

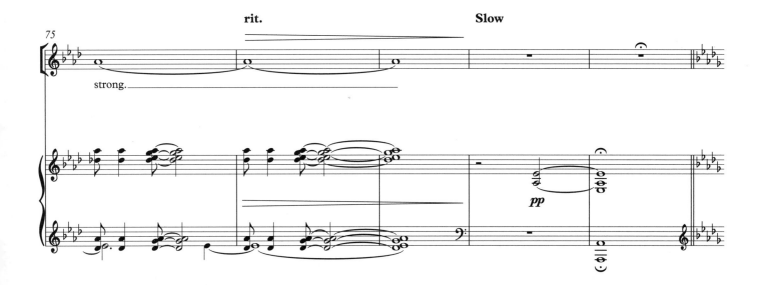

3. Apologia pro Poemate Meo

poco rit.

12

gave their laughs more glee than shakes a child, a child.

mp

a tempo

16

SOLO CELLO

p espress.

p espress.

I, too, have dropped off Fear, Be - hind the bar-rage, dead as my pla-

a tempo

p

20

mf

mf

-toon, And sailed my spi - rit surg-ing light and clear

mf

With the soft silk of eyes that look and long._____ I have per-ceived much beau-ty_____ In the hoarse oaths that kept our cour-age straight;_____ Heard mu - sic in the si - lent-ness of

du - ty;_____ Found peace where shell - storms

spout - ed red - dest spate,_____ found peace,_____ found__

peace,_____ found__ peace._____

rit.

rit.

4. Futility

nods._____ Save me,_____ save__ me,_____ save__

me._____

Save__ me,_____ save__ me._____

S. A.

Move him, move him in-to the sun,_____ the

T. B.

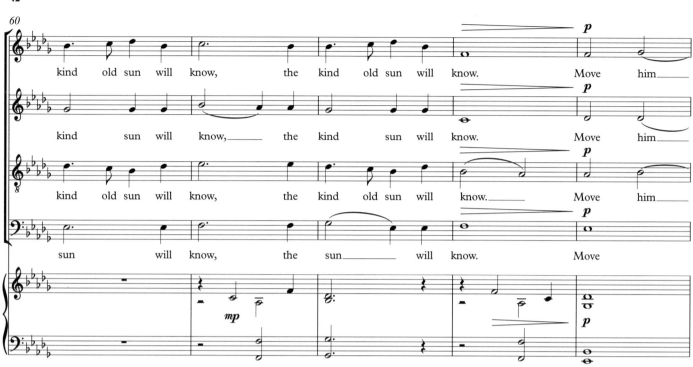

kind old sun will know, the kind old sun will know. Move him

kind sun will know, the kind sun will know. Move him

kind old sun will know, the kind old sun will know. Move him

sun will know, the sun will know. Move

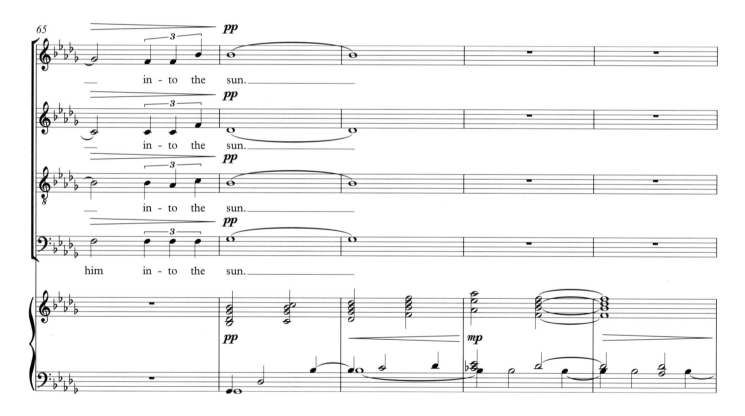

in - to the sun.

in - to the sun.

in - to the sun.

him in - to the sun.

Save____ me,____ save____ me.____

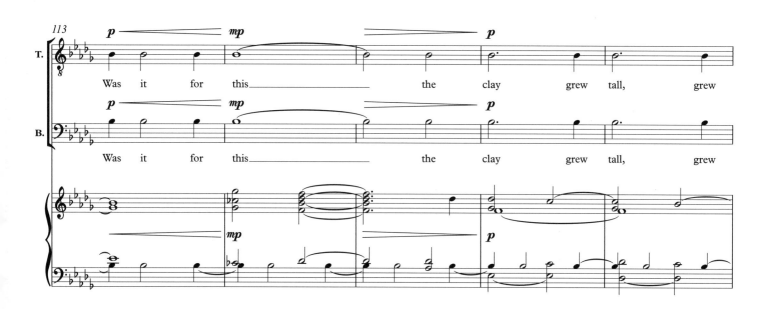

Was it for this_____ the clay grew tall, grew

Was it for this_____ the clay grew tall, grew

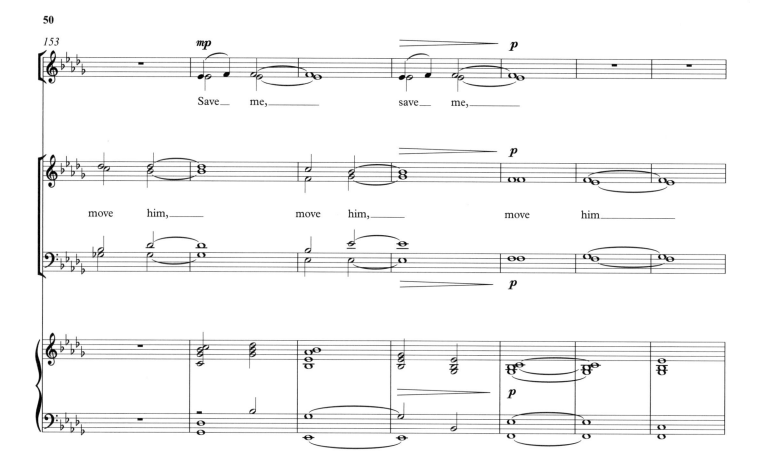

Save me, save me,
move him, move him, move him

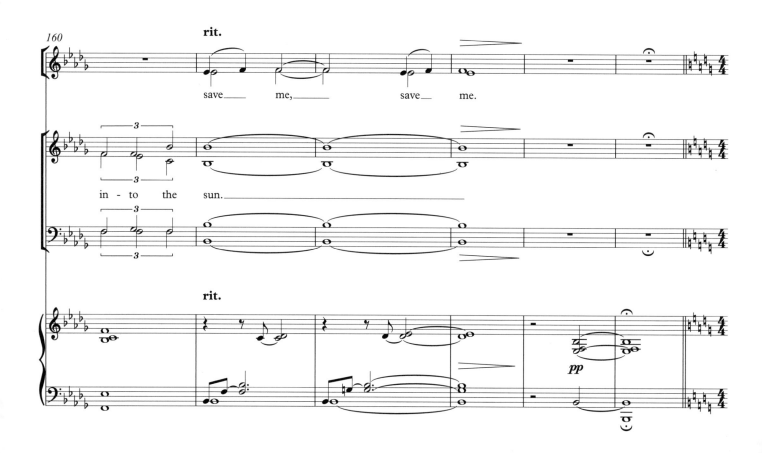

save me, save me.
in - to the sun.

5. Winter Song

Warm and lyrical ♩ = c.80

From off your face,_____ in - to the winds of win - ter,_____

The sun - brown and the sum - mer - gold are

blow - ing;_____ But they shall gleam a - gain with

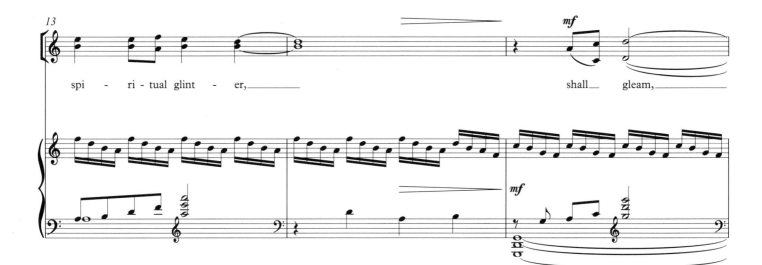

spi - ri - tual glint - er,_____ shall__ gleam,____ with

shall_____ gleam a - gain._____

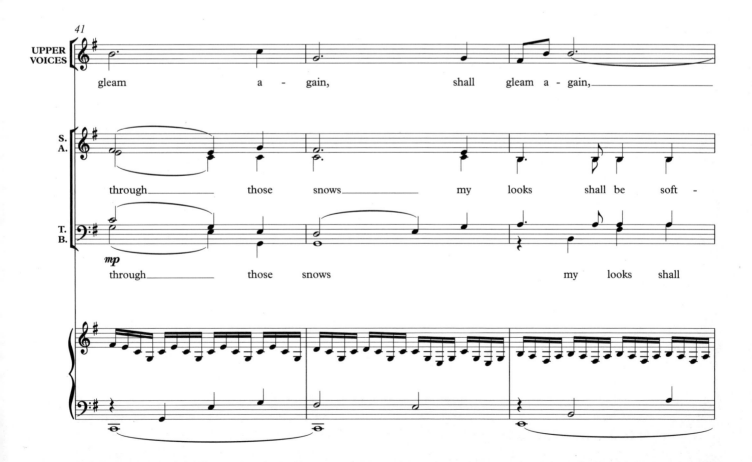

56

SNARE DRUM

2. Spring Offensive

BOB CHILCOTT

TENOR DRUM

2. Spring Offensive

BOB CHILCOTT

SOLO CELLO

3. *Apologia pro Poemate Meo*

BOB CHILCOTT